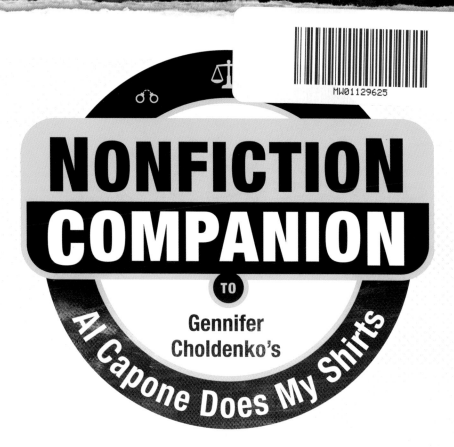

NONFICTION COMPANION

TO

Gennifer Choldenko's

Al Capone Does My Shirts

Lisa Kurkov

Educational Media

BEFORE, DURING, AND AFTER READING ACTIVITIES

Before Reading: Building Background Knowledge and Academic Vocabulary

Before Reading strategies activate prior knowledge and set a purpose for reading. Before reading a book, it is important to tap into what your child or students already know about the topic. This will help them develop their vocabulary and increase their reading comprehension.

Questions and activities to build background knowledge:
1. Look at the cover of the book. What will this book be about?
2. What do you already know about the topic?
3. Let's study the Table of Contents. What will you learn about in the book's chapters?
4. What would you like to learn about this topic? Do you think you might learn about it from this book? Why or why not?

Building Academic Vocabulary

Building academic vocabulary is critical to understanding subject content.
Assist your child or students to gain meaning of the following vocabulary words.

Content Area Vocabulary
Read the list. What do these words mean?

- apprehended
- autism
- bootlegging
- bribing
- consent
- convicts
- early intervention
- electroshock therapy
- infamous
- penitentiary
- savants
- soup kitchen

During Reading: Writing Component

During Reading strategies help to make connections, monitor understanding, generate questions, and stay focused.
1. While reading, write in your reading journal any questions you have or anything you do not understand.
2. After completing each chapter, write a summary of the chapter in your reading journal.
3. While reading, make connections with the text and write them in your reading journal.
   a) Text to Self – What does this remind me of in my life? What were my feelings when I read this?
   b) Text to Text – What does this remind me of in another book I've read? How is this different from other books I've read?
   c) Text to World – What does this remind me of in the real world? Have I heard about this before? (news, current events, school, etc.)

After Reading: Comprehension and Extension Activity

After Reading strategies provide an opportunity to summarize, question, reflect, discuss, and respond to the text. After reading the book, work on the following questions with your child or students to check their level of reading comprehension and content mastery.
1. What are two things Alcatraz has been? (Summarize)
2. Why do you think Alcatraz was turned into a prison? (Infer)
3. What do you think living on the island was like? (Asking Questions)
4. Moose's family drops everything to move. How would you have felt if you were Moose? (Text-to-Self Connection)

Extension Activity
Al Capone was a fascinating criminal, and people still talk about him today. Pick a book, article, or documentary and learn a little more about this famous crime boss.

TABLE OF CONTENTS

ABOUT *Al Capone Does My Shirts*

and **Gennifer Choldenko**

Al Capone Does My Shirts is a fictional story set in 1935 about Moose Flanagan and his family. They have just moved to Alcatraz, an island offshore from San Francisco, California, in the United States. It's hard enough to get used to a new school, let alone life on an island with a bunch of criminals. Moose has the added challenge of figuring out how to best help his sister, Natalie, who has **autism**.

Author Gennifer Choldenko is the youngest in her family and grew up with three older siblings, including a sister with autism. It was important to her to write honestly about that experience through the characters of Moose and Natalie. Choldenko got the idea for her Alcatraz books from a newspaper article she read. *Al Capone Does My Shirts* is the winner of 20 awards, including the Newbery Honor.

More Alcatraz, Please!

If you finished the novel and wished it weren't over yet, you're in luck! There are three more books in the Tales from Alcatraz series: Al Capone Shines My Shoes, Al Capone Does My Homework, *and* Al Capone Throws Me a Curve. *Choldenko has written 15 books but feels that the last of her Al Capone books is the best.*

SAN FRANCISCO, CA

THE ROCK

Alcatraz Island, also known as "the Rock," was named *Alcatraces* by Spanish explorer, Juan Manuel de Ayala. In Spanish, *alcatraces* means "pelicans," which are a type of seabird. Over time, the name changed to Alcatraz. The United States military used the island for about 80 years, until 1933, when the federal government opened a maximum-security prison there. The island was chosen, in part, because of its location. It is surrounded by the cold waters and strong currents of San Francisco Bay, and it lies approximately 1.25 miles (2 kilometers) from the mainland—a long, cold swim for any would-be escapees.

Did You Know?

- *The first U.S. Pacific Coast lighthouse, lit in 1854, was on Alcatraz.*
- *Alcatraz had a library with 15,000 books and about 75 magazine subscriptions.*
- *Beginning in the 1850s, Alcatraz was used as a military prison.*
- *While at Alcatraz, Al Capone played the banjo in a prison band called the Rock Islanders.*

CHILDREN OF ALCATRAZ

From the Novel

Most of the children, like Piper, relish the stranger aspects of life on the island. They enjoy showing around newcomers like Moose and Natalie. When they go to school on the mainland, they sometimes boast about where they live, but for the most part, their home feels like any small town of the era.

Children really did live on Alcatraz! The children who lived on the island had parents who worked at the prison. For the most part, Alcatraz was a pleasant place to grow up. The small size encouraged a tightly knit community; the kids played together and were in and out of each other's houses every day. The fact that 200 to 300 prisoners lived nearby wasn't an issue.

UNITED STATES PENITENTIARY

ALCATRAZ ISLAND | AREA 12 ACRES

$1\frac{1}{2}$ MILES TO TRANSPORT DOCK

ONLY GOVERNMENT BOATS PERMITTED

OTHERS MUST KEEP OFF 200 YARDS

NO ONE ALLOWED ASHORE

WITHOUT A PASS

BUILDING 46

Building 46 is where families lived on Alcatraz.

Reunion

Most of the kids who grew up on Alcatraz had such fond memories of their childhoods that they held alumni reunions once a year. Nearly 200 people would attend to share stories of life on the island. As the Alcatraz "kids" have aged, there aren't that many people left to attend the reunions. The last one was held in 2018, but the remaining alumni still keep in touch.

INSTITUTION
RULES & REGULATIONS

The Alcatraz kids saw inmates working around the island, and sometimes they'd wave or stop to chat. Occasionally, an alarm sounded, which signaled a riot or an escape, and meant the children had to head home immediately. It usually didn't cause anxiety among the children, although the adults would worry that a desperate prisoner might take a civilian hostage.

Families who lived on the island could leave whenever they wanted (as long as the ferry was running), but to get back on the island, they needed their dog tags to prove they lived there. And if a child wanted to have a friend over, they needed approval from the prison first. The friend then had to arrive via the ferry at a specific time.

WHAT IS AUTISM?

From the Novel

Although the Flanagan family doesn't have a name for Natalie's condition, they know her symptoms well. They know that some things make her life easier, and others usually make a situation worse. They desperately want to help her, but don't always know how.

AUTISTIC SPECTRUM CONDITION

Mild

Natalie's character is based on Choldenko's older sister, who has Autism Spectrum Disorder (ASD). It is called a spectrum disorder because those who are diagnosed fall somewhere on a broad spectrum. It can have a range of behaviors and can affect a person's life to varying degrees. Some people with ASD are mildly impacted by it. They need minimal supports to be successful in what they set out to do. Others are more severely affected. They require a more structured support system in order to live up to their full potential. Natalie's condition is based on one person and is not representative of the whole spectrum.

Severe

Difficulty with social skills is one sign of autism. Other common signs are repetitive behaviors, difficulty with speech and communication, and sensory issues, like being overwhelmed by loud noises, the way fabrics feel, or moving lights. Getting help early on, called **early intervention**, is very important. It can make communication and social interactions easier.

Daniel Paul Tammet is a mathematical savant, as well as a writer and essayist.

There is no known cause of autism. Experts believe it is the result of a combination of genetic and environmental factors. Some cases are quite severe, but autism does not hold people back. Many people who have autism or who were thought to have autism have lived very successful lives.

Savants with Autism

*Although it's relatively rare, some people with ASD are also **savants**. Savants have an extraordinary ability in a particular area, such as music, mathematics, or art. One example of a savant is Stephen Wiltshire, a British architectural artist. He couldn't speak until he was eight, but he can draw cityscapes down to the tiniest details!*

AUTISM NOW AND THEN

From the Novel

In the mid-1930s, when the novel takes place, scientists did not yet have a name and a diagnosis for autism. Moose and Natalie's mom desperately wants Natalie to be admitted to the Esther P. Marinoff school because she feels it's the best chance for Natalie to lead a "normal" life.

The Buffalo State Asylum (above) is an example of a place Natalie could have ended up living.

An actual definition of autism did not exist until 1943, when a child psychiatrist named Leo Kanner developed one. In the 1930s, young people like Natalie often ended up in asylums, where they were not likely to receive care that would actually help them. Treatment at these asylums varied. For example, **electroshock therapy**, or using electricity to induce seizures, was used to treat symptoms of autism in the 1930s.

Shocking Therapy Techniques

*Electroshock therapy did help some people, and it still does today. It is now called electroconvulsive therapy or ECT, and it uses mild electrical currents to stimulate certain parts of the brain. The differences between electroshock therapy then and now are large. With modern medicine, treatment is much more delicate and controlled. But the most important advancement is that patients can now **consent** to, or give permission for, the treatment—an option denied to many people in the past.*

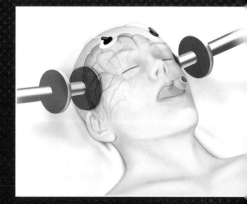

Autism symptoms and adaptive skills

COMPULSIVE BEHAVIOR

PRACTICAL SKILLS

RESTRICTED BEHAVIOR

SELF CARE

IGNORING THE DANGER

SOCIAL INTERACTION

REPETITIVE BEHAVIOR

COMMUNICATION

Today, we know much more about autism than ever before. Approximately 1 in 54 children in the U.S. are on the autism spectrum. Signs of autism are noticeable around the age of two, although many children are not diagnosed until four.

Because there is such a range of behavior within a diagnosis of ASD, the treatments also vary quite a bit. Applied behavior analysis (ABA) is the only research-based therapy for treating people with autism by encouraging positive behaviors and discouraging negative behaviors. Treatment helps people with autism communicate, build relationships, and be acting members of society.

CRIMINALS OF ALCATRAZ

From the Novel

When Theresa gives Moose a tour of the island on his first day, she gives him the lowdown on criminals housed there. She hands him a card with information about Al Capone, and then takes pride in telling him about other famous inmates, like "Machine Gun" Kelly and Roy Gardner.

U. S. PENITENTIARY
ALCATRAZ
1428
11 16 59

Whitey Bulger, an Irish American crime boss, was at Alcatraz in 1959.

From 1934 until 1963, Alcatraz was known for the toughest prisoners. Most prisoners were not sent directly to Alcatraz; instead, they made their way there through bad behavior. If they managed to avoid any incidents for about five years, they were sometimes sent back to lower security prisons.

Perks of Alcatraz

Although Alcatraz had a reputation for being remote, harsh, and inescapable, some prisoners actually wanted to go there. Inmates had individual cells at Alcatraz. The cells were small—about 9 feet by 5 feet—but prisoners had to worry less about personal safety. The food was also relatively good, since prisoners were less likely to riot if they were well fed.

MENU

Cream celery soup

Roast young turkey

Cranberry sauce

Saltine crackers

Vegetable dressing

Giblet gravy

Combination salad

Mayonnaise dressing

Creamed mash potatoes

Candied sweet potatoes

Asparagus tips on toast

White celery

Mixed sweet pickles

Chocolate layer cake

Walnut layer cake

Fruit cake

Miner pie

Bananas

Apples

Parker honey rolls

Coffee

Milk

Butter

Mixed Candies

Robert Stroud, "The Birdman of Alcatraz," was one of the most famous inmates. He was a violent and difficult prisoner, but he had a soft spot for birds. He was allowed to breed and study canaries at Leavenworth Prison, even running a lab inside two adjoining cells. He wrote two books about canaries and created bird medicines that he was allowed to sell. Despite his nickname, he never actually kept birds while at Alcatraz.

Roy Gardner, the last "Great American Train Robber," was another famous prisoner at Alcatraz. He was known for robbing banks and mail trains and had a reputation as a master escape artist. He managed to escape from the **penitentiary** at McNeil Island, but was later recaptured during another train robbery. Gardner was one of the first inmates to publish a memoir about his experiences at Alcatraz.

Robert Stroud, "The Birdman of Alcatraz"

AL CAPONE DOES CRIME

From the Novel

In the story, Al Capone has quite a reputation among the children on Alcatraz. They are aware of his celebrity and consider how it might be useful. Piper writes to Capone, asking for an autographed baseball, and Moose writes a letter in hopes that Capone can help get Natalie into the Esther P. Marinoff School.

Capone quit school after he hit a teacher when he was in sixth grade. He found success as a criminal at a young age when he joined a street gang. Later, he ran a nightclub and was involved in several shady operations, including gambling rings and **bootlegging**, or making and selling alcohol illegally.

Born in Brooklyn, Al Capone became the most **infamous** gangster in American history.

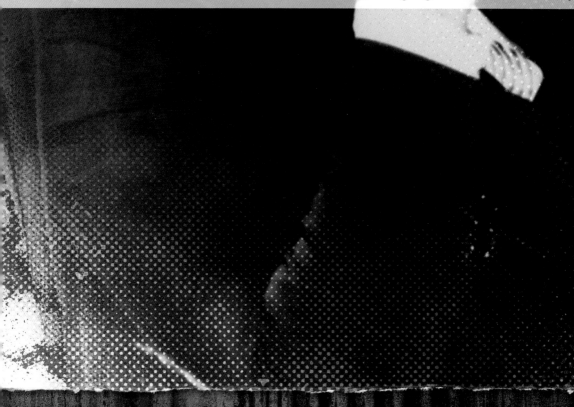

Capone became known as a powerful and violent Chicago gangster, whose empire was said to be worth more than $62 million by 1929. In 1929, Capone masterminded the St. Valentine's Day Massacre, a mass murder of seven members of a rival gang. President Herbert Hoover was determined to bring down the infamous mob boss. However, the FBI couldn't prove that Capone was responsible for the massacre. When he was finally sent to prison in 1931, it was because of tax evasion, not murder.

Al Capone funded the above soup kitchen in Chicago, Illinois.

Facts About Al Capone

- As a teen, he worked as a pinboy in a bowling alley.
- His nickname was Scarface, from several scars he got from a fight at age 21. He hated the name.
- He had a press secretary to help him keep a positive public image.
- He lobbied to have sell-by dates added to milk bottles.
- He funded a **soup kitchen** to provide meals to people during the Great Depression.

SPECIAL TREATMENT

From the Novel

In the novel, Alcatraz's warden was strict, rule-abiding, and didn't allow for any special treatment. This was a change for Al Capone, who was used to buying favors with his immense wealth and powerful connections.

Above is a recreation of Capone's cell at Eastern State Penitentiary. Below is his cell while he was in Alcatraz.

Al Capone transferred to Alcatraz from a prison in Atlanta. Authorities disliked the special treatment he received in Atlanta as a result of **bribing** the guards. His cell had carpeting, expensive bedding, and a radio, which he would listen to with the guards while they chatted. He received special meals, and most significantly, he was allowed to continue running his Chicago gangster operations from prison.

ESCAPE FROM
ALCATRAZ

When the warden asks to speak to Moose, he gives him a rundown on the island's rules. He tells Moose that the inmates are terrible men with nothing to do but sit around planning ways to escape. He enumerates the prisoners' track record for escapes (before they came to Alcatraz), and Moose wonders why on Earth women and children are allowed to live on the island.

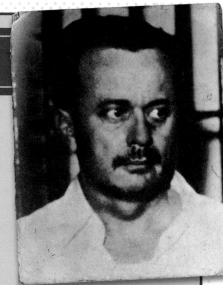

Arthur "Doc" Barker died trying to escape from Alcatraz.

Over the years that Alcatraz operated as a prison, there were 14 escape attempts involving 36 men. None of the attempts were successful, meaning that none of the men escaped and made it to freedom alive. The majority of escapees were caught, six were shot and killed, and two drowned. Five more were never found, so it is assumed that they also drowned.

ESCAPE

Shortest distance from Alcatraz to shore is 1.25 miles

Alcatraz Prison

Treasure Island

San Fransisco

Escape from Alcatraz Triathlon

In 1981, a new triathlon event was created called Escape from Alcatraz. It involves a 1.5-mile (2.4-kilometer) swim from Alcatraz Island, followed by an 18-mile (29-kilometer) bike ride and an 8-mile (12.8-kilometer) run. Athletes can complete the long, chilly, rough swim because they have trained in cold water, and the race is timed to avoid high tide.

USPA 79624 2 13 58

John William Anglin, FB

Frank Lee Morris
FBI #2 157 606
COPY

S

CLARENCE ANGLIN, DOB 5-11-31, age 31, Ht- 5'11½",
Wt- 168 lbs., build medium, eyes hazel, comp. light
tattoo: "Zona" left wrist; "Nita" right 4 arm.

Hole in cell.

Decoy heads

One of the largest escape attempts, called the Battle of Alcatraz, occurred in May of 1946. Six prisoners took control of the cellhouse and ended up battling with prison officials. Eighteen officers were hurt, and two were killed. Three of the escapees died, two were given the death sentence, and one received a second life sentence.

Frank Morris, John Anglin, and Clarence Anglin get credit for planning the most elaborate escape. Using sharpened spoons, they chipped away at the crumbling cell walls and made decoys to fool the guards into thinking that they were in their beds! The inmates used soap and plaster to make fake heads. They even added hair from the prison barbershop. With standard prisoner raincoats, the three men created a makeshift boat and sailed away. The escapees' possessions were found in the bay, but their bodies were never recovered. Could they have truly escaped?

Escape in Uniform

One creative escape attempt was made by prisoner John Giles in 1945. He worked with laundry at the loading dock and managed to steal a complete army uniform—slowly, one piece at a time so that it wouldn't be missed. He escaped onto a boat, but the boat was headed for Angel Island, a military base, rather than San Francisco, and he was quickly **apprehended**.

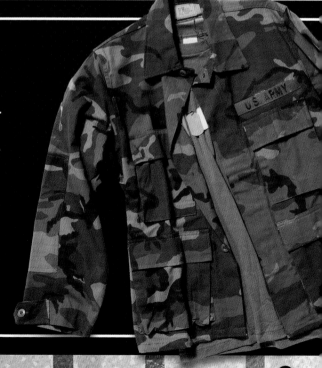

ON THE JOB

From the Novel

Moose is surprised when he first learns that **convicts** do the laundry on the island. It seems strange to him that he'll wear clothing that murderers and kidnappers have touched. Piper, who is used to prisoner-washed laundry, dreams up the plan of selling the Alcatraz laundry service to kids at school.

Prisoners could be assigned to a variety of jobs on the island. Some did basic cooking or cleaning in the cellhouse, while others did landscaping and gardening jobs or worked on the dock or in the library. The most common jobs, however, were factory-type jobs on the northwest end of the island. Inmates took care of laundry and dry cleaning for prisoners, nearby military personnel, and the island's families.

Prisoners also made items such as shoes, raincoats, gloves, and rubber mats. During World War II, like many businesses, the Alcatraz industrial buildings switched over to making items that helped the war effort, such as cargo nets and buoys.

The San Francisco area is known for its intense fog. On days when the fog was particularly heavy, inmates didn't have to go to work. It was too difficult for the guards to keep a close eye on prisoners during the walk through "pea soup" fog!

RUBE GOLDBERG MACHINES

When Moose first meets Jimmy Mattaman, Jimmy is working on a marble-shooting machine. It's a complicated machine, made of rocks, marbles, sticks, and rubber bands. Rube Goldberg machines were very popular at the time and are likely where Jimmy got his inspiration.

Rube Goldberg with his family.

Rube Goldberg was a cartoonist and inventor who may be best remembered for his comic strip *The Inventions of Professor Lucifer Gorgonzola Butts*, which ran from 1929 to 1931. The cartoons depicted silly contraptions that accomplished something simple via a complicated chain reaction. Today, there are all kinds of contests for students to design their own crazy machines that accomplish simple tasks.

Students test their own Rube Goldberg machine.

AMERICA'S FAVORITE PASTIME

From the Novel

The kids on Alcatraz enjoy playing baseball, as do the convicts. It's especially exciting when the inmates hit a ball over the fence and one of the kids retrieves it. The obsession with baseball on Alcatraz reflects the nation's love of the game during that difficult decade.

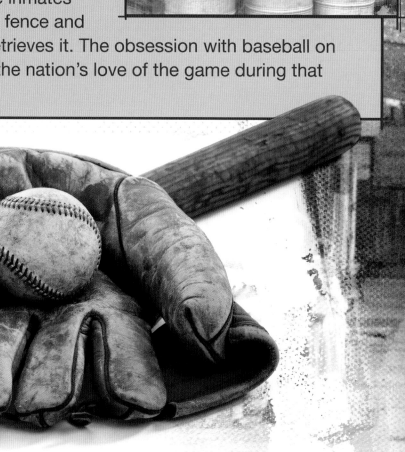

As the 1930s began, the U.S. had just entered the Great Depression. The country was still reeling from the stock market crash and increasing rates of unemployment. Baseball offered an escape from reality. Watching a game was exciting. It allowed the spectators to be in the moment, rooting for their team and celebrating victories or mourning defeats.

Attendance was down at games in the 30s because many people couldn't afford tickets, but listening on the radio and reading the newspapers the next day was an easy way to follow the action.

Baseball in the 1930s included some of the greatest stars of the game. The first year of the decade saw legends Babe Ruth and Lou Gehrig each hit more than 40 home runs. Joe DiMaggio began playing for the Yankees in 1935. Satchel Paige dominated in the Negro Leagues and was called the greatest pitcher in baseball by Ted Williams. Jobs were still hard to come by, many people didn't have enough to eat, and the economy was a mess . . . but there was always baseball.

On May 15, 1941, New York Yankees' slugger Joe DiMaggio's 56-game hitting streak began.

A Very Valuable Ball!

Babe Ruth and Al Capone were said to be buddies. In 1931, they signed the same baseball, right before Capone was sent to prison. Today, it is quite a collector's item. In 2013, it sold at auction for nearly $62,000!

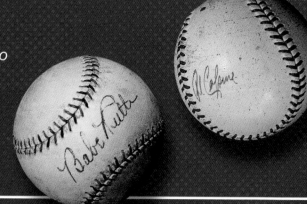

DISCUSSION QUESTIONS

1. Explain what a spectrum disorder is.

2. Why was escaping from Alcatraz nearly impossible?

3. Do you think you would have enjoyed growing up on Alcatraz? Why or why not?

4. Describe why a prisoner might hope for a transfer to Alcatraz.

5. Explain why baseball was such a popular pastime during the 1930s.

6. How has treatment for autism changed from the 1930s to today?

7. Were the prisoner strikes at Alcatraz successful? Explain.

Gabby Hartnett autographs a baseball for Sonny Capone, sitting with his father, Al Capone, at a Chicago Cubs baseball game.

WRITING PROMPTS AND PROJECTS

1. Write a letter to one of the Alcatraz prisoners—it can be to an inmate who was actually imprisoned there or to a fictional inmate. Think carefully about what you'd like to ask the prisoner about his crimes, life, and Alcatraz experiences.

2. Temple Grandin, an expert in animal behavior, has autism and is a noted autism advocate. Go to YouTube and search *Temple Grandin* and *CNN interview* to watch a short clip about what it's like to have autism. Do some more reading about Grandin, online or at the library. Then write a short essay on what you've learned about autism from Grandin.

3. Design your own Rube Goldberg-style machine. You can look up some of his inventions online first and then draw a sketch of your own version—or better yet, build a model!

4. Visit the author's website to read interviews with people who lived and worked on Alcatraz (www.alcaponedoesmyshirts.com/interviews/tag/). Make a list of at least four more questions you'd like to ask the interviewees if you could.

5. Detailed Project: Do some research, at the library or online, about baseball in the 1930s.

    *   On a piece of poster board, create a timeline showing the highlights.

    *   If you'd like, you can print out images you find online to illustrate your timeline.

    *   Share your timeline with classmates, friends, or family.

GLOSSARY

apprehended (ap-ri-HEND-id): caught; taken into custody

autism (AW-tiz-uhm): a developmental disorder marked by difficulty with communication

bootlegging (BOOT-leg-ing): making and selling alcohol illegally

bribing (brahyb-ing): making a payment to someone in exchange for a favor or a service

consent (kuhn-SENT): to agree to or give approval for something that is done

convicts (KAAN-vikts): people who are serving a, usually long, prison sentence

early intervention (UR-lee in-ter-VEN-shuhn): support and services for young children who have developmental delays of various types

electroshock therapy (ih-LEK-truh-shok ther-UH-pee): the treatment of mental illness by applying electrical currents to the head

infamous (IN-fuh-muhs): having a bad reputation

penitentiary (pen-i-TEN-shu-ree): a state or federal prison

savants (sa-VAHNTS): people who have a developmental disorder but also have an extraordinary skill

soup kitchen (soop KICH-uhn): a place where people in need can receive a free meal

BIBLIOGRAPHY

Alcatraz History. www.alcatrazhistory.com. (accessed July 31, 2020).

Baby Professor. *Al Capone: A Dangerous Existence*. Newark: Speedy Publishing LLC, 2017.

Biography.com Editors. "Al Capone Biography." Last updated May 11, 2020. www.biography.com/crime-figure/al-capone.

Choldenko, Gennifer. *Al Capone Does My Shirts: A Tale from Alcatraz*. New York: Penguin Group, 2004.

Fattig, Michelle. "Famous People Who Have or Had Asperger's Syndrome." *Disabled World*, Disabled World, 19 Jan. 2020, www.disabled-world.com/disability/awareness/famous/asp.php. (accessed August 18, 2020).

Gennifer Choldenkow. ww.choldenko.com. (accessed July 28, 2020).

Gouldsberry, Eric. "The 1930's: The Dog Days of the Depression." https://thisgreatgame.com/1930s-baseball-history/. (accessed August 4, 2020).

History.com Editors. "Alcatraz." Last updated June 7, 2019. www.history.com/topics/crime/alcatraz.

MegEvans. "About Autism." *Autistic Self Advocacy Network*, autisticadvocacy.org/about-asan/about-autism/. (accessed August 2, 2020).

Roth, Kristyn, and Molly Gustafson. "Home." *Autism Society*, 24 Oct. 2016, www.autism-society.org/. (accessed August 2, 2020).

INDEX TERMS

ABOUT THE AUTHOR

Lisa Kurkov lives in Charlotte, North Carolina, where she and her husband homeschool their two children. When her head isn't buried in a book, Lisa enjoys baking, crafting, photography, birding, and adventuring with her family.

© 2021 Rourke Educational Media

All rights reserved. No part of this book may be reproduced or utilized in any form or by any means, electronic or mechanical including photocopying, recording, or by any information storage and retrieval system without permission in writing from the publisher.

www.rourkeeducationalmedia.com

PHOTO CREDITS: page 1: Denisfilm/ Getty Images; page 2: cgdeaw/ Getty Images; page 4: bluejayphoto/ Getty Images; page 5: AliLooney/ Getty Images; page 6: Danita Delimont Photography/Newscom; page 7: akg-images/Newscom; page 7: FrankRampott/ Getty Images; page 8: Luca_Boveri; page 8: H. Armstrong Roberts/ Getty Images; page 8: Pabkov/ Shutterstock.com; page 9: FatCamera/ Getty Images; page 10: Cindy Miller Hopkins / DanitaDelimont.com "Danita Delimont Photography"/Newscom; page 10: Tim Wagner/ZUMAPRESS/Newscom; page 12: Viktoriia Sytnik/ Getty Images; page 12: ktaylorg/ Getty Images; page 12: khalus/ Getty Images; page 13: malerapaso/ Getty Images; page 13: art_of_sun/ Shutterstock.com; page 14: PHOTOPQR/OUEST FRANCE; page 14: BRENDAN MCDERMID/REUTERS/Newscom; page 14: Roman Yanushevsky/Shutterstock.com; page 15: Bryan Smith/ZUMA Press/Newscom; page 15: Bryan Smith/ZUMA Press/Newscom; page 16: ilbusca/ Getty Images; page 17: tBSIP/Newscom; page 17: AnkiHoglund/ Getty Images; page 17: gremlin/ Getty Images; page 18: vejaa/ Getty Images; page 18: ktaylorg/ Getty Images; page 19: AlexeyBlogoodf/ Getty Images; page 19: David Wong/SCMP/Newscom; page 20: akg-images/Newscom; page 20: Everett Collection/Newscom; page 20: FBI/ZUMAPRESS/Newscom; page 20: My Colorful Past / Mediadrumworl; page 22: Lisa Hoffner / DanitaDelimont.com "Danita Delimont Photography"/Newscom; page 23:Everett Collection/Newscom; page 23:Jules Annan/ZUMA Press/Newscom; page 24: Iulia Suciu/Shutterstock.com; page 25: UPPA/Photoshot/Newscom; page 26: Album/Newscom; page 27: Everett Collection/Newscom; page 28: Parrot Pascal/ABACA/Newscom; page 28: Ryan Noble/ZUMAPRESS/Newscom; page 29: Weird NJ / Splash News/Newscom; page 30: Everett Collection/Newscom; page 31: FrankRampott/ Getty Images; page 31: tomch/ Getty Images; page 31: Aric Crabb/MCT/Newscom; page 32: Everett Collection/Newscom; page 32: diane39/ Getty Images; page 32: Ferrari/ZUMA Press/ Newscom; page 32: Ferrari/ZUMA Press/Newscom; page 32: Ferrari/ZUMA Press/Newscom; page 32: Ferrari/ZUMA Press/Newscom; page 33: Thomas Northcut/ Getty Images; page 34: Lisa Hoffner / DanitaDelimont.com "Danita Delimont Photography"/Newscom; page 35: akg-images/ Newscom; page 35: akg-images/Newscom; page 36: Spondylolithesis/ Getty Images; page 36: Alex Milan Tracy/Sipa USA/Newscom; page 37: Sergiy1975/ Getty Images; page 38: Everett Collection/Newscom; page 38: KRT/Newscom; page 39: Paul Yeung/SCMP/Newscom; page 40: eurobanks/ Getty Images; page 40: Staff/Mirrorpix/Newscom; page 41: Lewis W. Hine Glasshouse Images/Newscom; page 42: Everett Collection/Newscom; page 43: KIMBERLY WHITE/REUTERS/Newscom; page 44: Everett Collection/Newscom; cover: Album/Newscom; cover: Lisa Hoffner / DanitaDelimont.com "Danita Delimont Photography"/Newscom; cover: natthanim/ Getty Images; cover: AliLooney/ Getty Images; cover: Tolga TEZCAN/ Getty Images; cover: Tolga TEZCAN/ Getty Images; cover: bluejayphoto/ Getty Images; cover: Armstrong Roberts/ Getty Images; cover: GLYPHstock/ Gtty Images; cover: Denisfilm/ Getty Images; cover: cgdeaw/ Getty Images; n/a: enjoynz/ Getty Images; n/a: slav-/ Getty Images

Library of Congress PCN Data

Nonfiction Companion to Gennifer Choldenko's Al Capone Does My Shirts / Lisa Kurkov
(Nonfiction Companions)
ISBN 978-1-73164-343-8 (hard cover)
ISBN 978-1-73164-307-0 (soft cover)
ISBN 978-1-73164-407-7 (e-Pub)
ISBN 978-1-73164-375-9 (e-Book)
Library of Congress Control Number: 2020945032

Rourke Educational Media
Printed in the United States of America
01-3502011937

Edited by: Madison Capitano
Cover and interior design by: Joshua Janes